TEEN CHALLENGES

BODY IMAGE AND DYSMORPHIA

by A. W. Buckey

CONTENT CONSULTANT

D. C. Walker
Clinical Psychologist
Assistant Professor of Psychology, Union College
Schenectady, New York

Essential Library

An Imprint of Abdo Publishing | abdobooks.com

ABDOBOOKS.COM

Published by Abdo Publishing, a division of ABDO, PO Box 398166, Minneapolis, Minnesota 55439. Copyright © 2022 by Abdo Consulting Group, Inc. International copyrights reserved in all countries. No part of this book may be reproduced in any form without written permission from the publisher. Essential Library™ is a trademark and logo of Abdo Publishing.

Printed in the United States of America, North Mankato, Minnesota.
102021
012022

THIS BOOK CONTAINS RECYCLED MATERIALS

Cover Photos: Krakenimages.com/Shutterstock Images, foreground; Shutterstock Images, background
Interior Photos: DGL Images/iStockphoto, 4; Leo Patrizi/iStockphoto, 8; Jaren Jai Wicklund/Shutterstock Images, 12–13; Odua Images/Shutterstock Images, 14; Shutterstock Images, 19, 34, 45, 56, 80–81; Kumi Komini/iStockphoto, 23; ProStock Studio/Shutterstock Images, 24; Delmaine Donson/iStockphoto, 31; iStockphoto, 36, 65, 68, 76, 87; LightField Studios/Shutterstock Images, 40; Rawpixel.com/Shutterstock Images, 42–43; Alexander Image/Shutterstock Images, 46; Dusan Petkovic/Shutterstock Images, 50; BSIP/Universal Images Group/Getty Images, 53; Christopher Morris/Corbis Sport/Getty Images, 59; Sthanlee B. Mirador/Sipa USA/AP Images, 66; Dmytro Zinkevych/Shutterstock Images, 73; David Mack/Science Source, 75; Deepak Sethi/iStockphoto, 82; Mariia Boiko/Shutterstock Images, 89; Elena Rostunova/Shutterstock Images, 92; Gonzalo Marroquin/Aerie/Getty Images Entertainment/Getty Images, 96; Richard Shotwell/Invision/AP Images, 98

Editor: Megan Ellis
Series Designer: Colleen McLaren

LIBRARY OF CONGRESS CONTROL NUMBER: 2021941209

PUBLISHER'S CATALOGING-IN-PUBLICATION DATA

Names: Buckey, A. W., author.

Title: Body image and dysmorphia / by A. W. Buckey

Description: Minneapolis, Minnesota : Abdo Publishing, 2022 | Series: Teen challenges | Includes online resources and index.

Identifiers: ISBN 9781532196256 (lib. bdg.) | ISBN 9781098218065 (ebook)

Subjects: LCSH: Body image in adolescence--Juvenile literature. | Body image--Social aspects--Juvenile literature. | Self-acceptance in adolescence--Juvenile literature. | Body image disturbance--Juvenile literature. | Psychology, Pathological--Juvenile literature.

Classification: DDC 306.4--dc23

CONTENTS

People with negative body image may have a difficult time finding motivation to start their day.

CHAPTER ONE

THE PERSON IN THE MIRROR

Max snoozes his alarm for the third time, but he doesn't fall back asleep. He rolls over onto his back and blinks up at the ceiling. He feels tired and anxious, like he overslept and underslept at the same time. The alarm starts blaring again, and Max sighs as he shuts it off.

Before he leaves his room, he does 50 push-ups and 50 squats next to his bed as part of his morning routine. But even though he's finished his routine, Max still dreads the enemy he has to face as he goes to take a shower: the bathroom mirror.

Lately, Max can't help but spend hours and hours in front of the mirror looking at his arms, legs, torso, and chest. Every day he finds something new that's wrong with his body. Even though he's been doing the extra push-ups and squats for a couple weeks now, Max frowns as he twists around to look at his shoulders and back. It doesn't look like anything has changed. The last time he went to the doctor, everything was completely normal—

normal height, normal weight, perfect health. Still, Max can't stop obsessing over something he doesn't have. Why can't he be more muscular?

Max runs downstairs to grab breakfast. His sister offers him some pancakes, Max's favorite, but his dad seems happy when Max quickly scrambles some egg whites instead. Max comes from a family that values athleticism—his mom and dad met on their college swim team, and his dad was even an amateur bodybuilder for a few years. Growing up, he got the message that muscular men were more powerful and better looking than guys who were less buff. In the video games he played, heroes were tall, with visible muscles and very little fat on their bodies. And in the superhero movies Max and his dad watched together, all the heroes were large and muscular too.

FAMILY MEALS AND BODY IMAGE

According to a 2019 study, teens in families that regularly eat breakfast together were more likely to have a healthy body image. Daily breakfast is a healthy habit for teens. Regularly eating breakfast helps improve energy and concentration. The authors of the study supposed that taking time to eat together can allow caregivers to model healthy and regular eating as well as provide caregivers opportunities to discuss body image and show interest in their children's lives.

Max has always been a little shorter than average, with a slender frame. But he's an athlete, just like his parents. He likes to run. He's good at it, and last year he even made the cross-country team. It's given him plenty of preparation to sprint out the door as his friend Shayna honks one final time from the driveway.

Shayna gives Max a ride to school every morning, but she never waits for him if he's late. He makes it just in time, and she raises her eyebrows at him suspiciously when he gets in the car. "Everything OK?" she asks.

"Yeah," Max says, pulling out his water bottle from his backpack. "Just couldn't stop snoozing my alarm."

Shayna puts on their favorite album, and even though she usually sings along, she's quiet the entire way to school. Max raises *his* eyebrows at *her*. "What about you?" he asks. "Are you OK?"

She sighs. "I don't know if I'm going to try out for cross-country again this year," she says. "I've been nervous to tell you."

Max is shocked. "Really? But you love running."

> "LEARNING TO BE GRATEFUL FOR OUR BODIES AND TAKING CARE OF THEM ARE THE BEST WAYS FOR US TO EMPOWER OURSELVES PHYSICALLY, MENTALLY, AND SPIRITUALLY."[1]
>
> —*DEMI LOVATO, SINGER*

People of all body types can enjoy active exercise.

"I'm tired of all the meets, and I want more free afternoons," Shayna says, but she doesn't look at Max.

Max wonders whether that's the real reason or whether it's because Shayna doesn't get along with the other girls on the team. Shayna had driven home crying from a meet last year because one of her teammates had told Shayna she was too fat to be a good runner. Even though Shayna outran that teammate during the meet, the words hurt.

"Yeah, the schedule can be intense," Max says. He doesn't want to push it. "I've been thinking I might take up weight lifting this year instead. My dad has some weights in the garage I can use."

Shayna looks shocked. "Really? But you hate lifting weights."

Max shrugs. Running isn't going to help him get buff, and he doesn't know how many more mornings he can stand looking at his tiny body in the bathroom mirror. "I figure it might be good for me," he says, and Shayna leaves it at that.

Before his first class, Max slips into an empty bathroom and lifts up his shirt to look at his abs. His stomach is a little more filled out than it was earlier in the morning. Even though Max knows that it's natural because he ate breakfast, the sight of his ab-free stomach makes him feel nauseated. The bell rings, and Max curses under his breath as he sprints off to class.

Max manages to stay awake through all his morning classes. Lunch is kind of awkward. He has to spend the first ten minutes trying to find an empty bathroom so he can check the mirror again. Once he's home, it's an hour in the garage gym, a shower, and then some time back in front of the mirror, flexing and inspecting his body. His mom makes meat loaf for dinner, but Max makes some pasta for himself too, wanting to bulk up. At night, he sits in front of his laptop and tries to work up the energy to do his homework. He knows he's not the only one of his friends who feels unsatisfied with his body. But he's felt so anxious and out of touch with himself lately. He wonders whether what he's going through is normal. Max puts off his paper for a little while longer. Instead, he opens his laptop and Googles: "When do you hate your body too much?"

WEIGHT LOSS AND SOCIAL MEDIA

Many companies post sponsored content and ads to Instagram and other social media sites, including companies that make weight loss items such as teas and pills. One company, Flat Tummy Co., became especially good at marketing its products through sponsored content. The company would pay celebrities and influencers with thin or athletic bodies to post about how the tea had helped them lose weight. At one point, the company was trying to recruit more than 50 new influencers a week.[2] In reality, the tea contains a laxative that can be dangerous if used repeatedly. In 2019, Instagram announced a policy that shielded users younger than 18 from seeing the ads. However, people older than 18 can still see these ads in their feeds.

NEGATIVE BODY IMAGE

Max's search takes him to some interesting places. He learns that negative body image is common and it can be unhealthy. He reads about guys who get so obsessed with becoming more muscular that it takes over their lives. Some articles identify it as muscle dysmorphia, a type of body dysmorphic disorder (BDD). BDD is a serious mental disorder. Max doesn't know whether he has this disorder, but he feels a connection to the symptoms and stories that he reads online. Max decides to confide in Shayna about the struggles he's been having. He hopes that she'll understand.

When Max talks to Shayna that night, she suggests he should open up to his parents. He decides to follow her advice. Though at first he has a hard time talking about his feelings, afterward he feels a sense of relief. Max's parents encourage him to talk to his doctor about these feelings, and they make a plan to find a therapist in the area who works with teens and body image.

Max's question is one a lot of teens ask. The teen years are times of huge personal changes, physically, mentally, and emotionally. Teens spend a lot of time figuring out who they want to be and adjusting to their bodies as they grow and change. Amid all this change, family, social groups, and society as a whole send out messages about how bodies should look and which kinds of bodies are most desirable.

"I TRY TO ONLY WORK IN SPACES NOW THAT MAKE ME FEEL COMFORTABLE. IT'S CHALLENGING, BUT I'D RATHER BE HEALTHY AND HAPPY AND LOVE MY BODY."[3]
—AMANDLA STENBERG, ACTRESS

It's not surprising that body image can be complicated. A 2015 US study found that in data gathered in the early 2000s, about 25 percent of teen boys said they wished they were leaner and more muscular.[4] In 2015, nearly 80 percent of US teen girls reported being unhappy with their bodies by age 17.[5] Teens are at high risk of developing BDD, which affects approximately two percent of people in the United States.[6] People with BDD become so troubled by their appearance that these feelings have a significant, negative effect on their daily lives. For example, they may not leave the house for days because they are concerned about their appearance.

For others who do not have BDD, negative body image can impair mental and physical health, relationships, quality of life, and self-esteem. Negative body image is a common problem for teens, but it doesn't have to be. Across the country, educators, influencers, and teens themselves are working to create a culture in which all kinds of bodies are accepted, celebrated, and deemed attractive.

Teens with BDD may feel uncomfortable in various situations such as public events, school, or work.

A person's body image begins developing as an infant.

CHAPTER TWO

HOW BODY IMAGE FORMS

Infants are born with a very basic understanding of their bodies. This helps them seek out food and respond to touch. As infants grow, they improve this understanding when they look at their hands or try to chew their own feet, coming to an understanding that their body parts belong to a whole.

According to psychologist Philippe Rochat, children develop the ability to recognize and understand themselves in stages, from birth to around age five. By the time they are about 18 months old, children have developed the self-awareness to recognize themselves in a mirror. It takes longer, however, for them to realize that the reflection they see is also a reflection of how others see them, and that they look that way all the time. This level of understanding occurs when children are around five years old.[1]

As they grow, children think about their own bodies and the bodies of others. They begin to take in messages from family and community members, and from the things they watch and hear, about how bodies are supposed to look and function. As kids apply these messages to their own bodies and senses of self, they develop attitudinal body image. The term "body image" often refers to attitudinal body image, the collection of thoughts, beliefs, and feelings about one's body. Research shows that attitudinal body image also develops in early childhood, although it continues to change throughout the course of a person's life.

Behavioral body image refers to the way people decide to treat their bodies. Key daily habits such as diet, exercise, and grooming routines help make up this behavioral body image. Elements of body image, body awareness, and self-awareness also work together. For example, a teen girl whose attitude toward her body is that she is too tall might start to slouch as a way to feel more comfortable with her looks.

TOYS AND BODY IMAGE

Children's dolls can reflect and shape body standards. Sometimes, these standards are greatly exaggerated in kids' toys. Barbie, for example, is one of the most famous dolls in US history. She's known for taking on a wide variety of jobs, identities, and styles throughout the years. One thing that had stayed the same, however, was her thin and curvy figure. A 2013 analysis of Barbie's body found that her waist was so small, and her wrists, ankles, and neck so long and thin, that a real-life woman with her shape would barely be able to survive. In response to criticism, Mattel, the company that makes Barbie toys, began making dolls of multiple body sizes in the 2010s.

BODY IMAGE MESSAGES

Children get their earliest messages about body image from their family members. According to social work professor and body image expert Janet Liechty, preschool-aged children are already absorbing ideas about things like preferred body size from their parents and other family members. Liechty led a study of two- to four-year-old children and their parents. Researchers asked the parents whether their children thought much about their bodies. The parents did not think their children understood issues about body image. However, when surveyed, "40 percent of the parents described their child exhibiting at least one body-related behavior, such as discussing weight, imitating comments about size or weight, or seeking praise for their appearance or clothing."[2]

Parenting style, or the way parents relate to their kids, can impact how kids approach their bodies. This impact can be positive or negative. For example, according to research in the *Journal of Youth and Adolescence*, parents who are typically "nurturing and warm"

"AS A PARENT OF PRESCHOOLERS, IT WAS EMPOWERING FOR ME TO REALIZE THAT BODY IMAGE IS BEING FORMED IN THESE EARLY YEARS."[3]

—JULIE BIRKY, COUNSELOR AND BODY IMAGE RESEARCHER

with their children are more likely to raise teens who are satisfied with their bodies.[4]

Children's experiences with their peers—friends, classmates, and siblings—also help shape their body image. Those who are victims of bullying at a young age are more likely to develop serious problems with body image later in life. This is especially true if the teasing is based on appearance. Peer influence tends to grow over time. By the time they reach sixteen years old, teens tend to spend more time with friends and classmates than with their parents. Dating and romantic relationships add a new dimension to body image concerns. Older kids and young teens often want to be attractive to potential partners. Children and teens tend to reinforce the messages they receive from media, advertising, and culture as a whole. These sources uphold beauty standards about how people's bodies should look.

BEAUTY STANDARDS

Beauty standards take the natural diversity of human body types and features and single out a few as especially desirable. For example, in US culture today, many people desire straight, white teeth because they represent a beauty standard. Beautiful people are expected to have straight, white teeth. People whose teeth don't fit that standard are encouraged to "fix" them in some way.

Children often mimic beauty standards they see represented in media, such as young girls playing with makeup.

US culture communicates this standard in a variety of ways. Boys and girls tend to look to celebrities like athletes, actors, and performers as examples of perfect bodies. Celebrities, models, and other public figures are likely to have straight, white teeth. In fact, it's common for actors and models whose teeth aren't naturally "perfect" to pay for teeth that fit this standard. One common fix involves shaving off parts of the tooth and putting in fake porcelain teeth, or veneers, on top of the tooth surface. Veneers have been popular with Hollywood celebrities since the 1990s, and many celebrities, including Cardi B and Hilary Duff, have gotten them. According to cosmetic dentist Michael Apa, veneers are now popular with Instagram celebrities and influencers. When famous people tend to have straight, white teeth, it sends a clear message that having similar teeth is an important part of being attractive.

Businesses and advertising firms do their part to promote society's beauty standards too. According to the firm Hexa Research, by 2024, the global tooth whitening market will be worth $7.4 billion.[5] Whitening toothpastes, at-home whitening kits and strips, and in-person bleaching treatments all promise whiter teeth in exchange for money. Advertising campaigns push the idea that whiter teeth

SIBLINGS AND BODY IMAGE

Siblings help model and reinforce ideas about body image. Even though siblings grow up with similar familial messages about body image, they can end up feeling very differently about their bodies. Some siblings may feel competitive over issues of beauty and body image. One 2016 study found evidence that sibling birth order can influence body feelings. The study focused on nine- to 12-year-old kids who had siblings. It found that older brothers were the most likely to make negative weight-related comments to siblings, while older sisters were the least likely.[6]

are better. A 2016–2017 ad campaign by Crest Whitestrips called the "tissue test" told the story of a woman who was embarrassed to find that her teeth were yellower than a piece of paper tissue, suggesting that other people should feel the same way.[7]

Straight, white teeth can be status symbols as well as signals of wealth and power. Most people don't naturally have perfectly straight teeth that pass the tissue test. Getting braces to align teeth typically costs thousands of dollars. Dental veneers are even more expensive, costing as much as $4,000 for just one tooth.[8] Professionally straightened and whitened teeth are

THE HISTORY OF BODY POSITIVITY

The term body positivity first emerged from the HIV/AIDS movement of the 1990s. Society often stigmatized those living with HIV or AIDS. Body positivity helped people living with AIDS embrace their bodies in the face of illness and discrimination. In 1996, body image activist Connie Sobczak and social worker Elizabeth Scott created a nonprofit that used the term in a different way. Their goal was to found a community for people looking to embrace self-love and eliminate feelings of body hatred. Many of Sobczak and Scott's ideas about body positivity came from the fat acceptance movement. That movement, which had been around since the 1960s, called for fat people to resist discrimination and love themselves as they are.

similar to designer clothes—signs that the person who has them can afford to spend money.

Beauty standards can seem completely natural and universal. When every attractive person on TV has straight teeth, and people talk about teeth whitening all the time, it feels obvious that everyone wants a certain type of teeth. But beauty standards change a great deal over space and time. In the United Kingdom, for example, some people find the US preference for very white teeth unnatural and unattractive. Some Japanese women pay to have their teeth made slightly crooked, with sharp canines that look a little like fangs. The trend is known as *yaeba,* and the crooked teeth are seen by some as cuter than straight ones. This diversity of beauty standards applies to all aspects of human appearance. Beauty standards are not only powerful and influential but also subjective and highly changeable.

> "WHOM WE DEEM 'BEAUTIFUL' IS A REFLECTION OF OUR VALUES."[9]
> —ROBIN GIVHAN, FASHION CRITIC

WHAT IS A HEALTHY BODY IMAGE?

There's no one way to have a healthy attitude toward your own body. However, healthy body image does have a few necessary ingredients. People with healthy body image

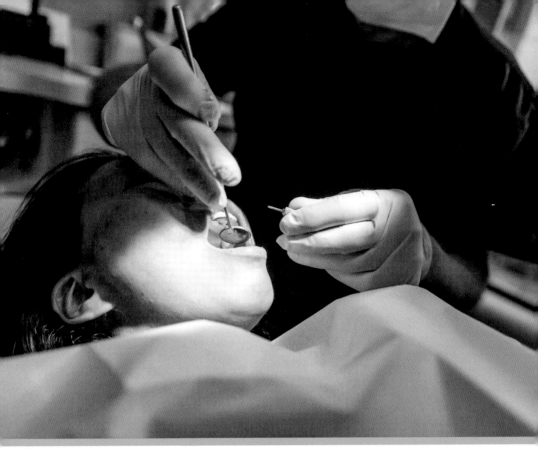

Some Japanese women undergo dental procedures to make their teeth intentionally crooked as part of a beauty trend.

have an accurate understanding of what their body looks like and how it moves. They feel at ease in their bodies and don't feel the need to spend too much time checking their appearance. And people with healthy body image tend to feel positive about or accepting toward their bodies. People with unhealthy body image struggle with one or both of these attitudes. Though unhealthy body image is very common in the United States, it is possible for someone with unhealthy body image to develop a healthier relationship with his or her body over time.

Teens receive many negative messages about body image from the media.

CHAPTER THREE

BODY IMAGE AND TEENS

People have unique relationships with their bodies. The strict, often unrealistic beauty standards of modern US culture can be nearly impossible for teens to ignore. Research shows that the majority of teen girls and many teen boys struggle with negative thoughts about their bodies. Beauty standards tend to vary across social categories such as gender and race, and they can promote inequality. While people throughout history have wrestled with body image and beauty standards, today's teens have to deal with the relatively new pressures of social media.

According to research compiled by psychologist Jake Linardon in 2015, approximately 50 percent of 13-year-old girls reported having a negative body image. And by age 17, 80 percent of girls disliked their bodies.[1] Many teens report that this dislike tends to stem from unhappiness with their weight. Thinness is one of the most powerful beauty standards in US culture. Americans are taught to associate thinness with beauty, health, and morality. People who aren't thin are shamed and encouraged to lose weight, and people who are thin are told to work hard to avoid gaining weight. For this reason, discussions of body image often center around issues of size and weight. In fact, 80 percent of teen girls in the United States say they are afraid to become fat, and by 17 years old, almost 90 percent have tried dieting.[2]

BODY IMAGE AND GENDER

Gender differences in body image and perception begin at a young age and continue throughout life. Teen girls tend to feel more negatively about their bodies than teen boys do, and they are significantly more likely to say that they often think about how they look. This trend continues into adulthood.

"OUR SOCIETY *DOES* REWARD BEAUTY ON THE OUTSIDE OVER HEALTH ON THE INSIDE."[3]
—*NAOMI WOLF, THE BEAUTY MYTH*

There are two main reasons that unhealthy body image tends to affect women more than men. First, beauty standards for girls and women are stricter and more numerous than those for boys and men. For example, a lot of teens get facial acne. Many teens with acne seek out special face washes or medications to deal with breakouts. But girls are often additionally encouraged—or expected—to hide their acne under makeup such as primer, foundation, powder, and concealer. The expectation that women should spend more time, energy, and money than men to meet beauty expectations is a double standard.

Second, there's a very old, sexist idea in Western culture that equates a woman's looks with her value as a human being. In an influential book, author Naomi Wolf called this idea the *beauty myth*. The beauty myth, Wolf explains, tells girls and women that they should always strive to be more beautiful.[4] The myth also teaches society that people can judge women by their looks when they do not judge men the same way. Wolf believes the beauty myth makes women less powerful by keeping them distracted with thoughts about their bodies. Even women who don't care about their looks can be hurt by the expectation that their appearance is everybody's business. For example, body image expert and psychologist Renee Engeln analyzed

THE PINK TAX

Society expects girls and women to pay for beauty products and grooming rituals that are not typical for men. However, even on products that both men and women use, women often pay more money for the same products. For example, disposable razors for men and women are almost identical, but women's versions tend to cost more than the men's versions. This phenomenon is known as the pink tax. A 2015 study of the pink tax in New York found that, on average, personal care products for women were 13 percent more expensive than personal products for men.[5]

studies that showed that even neutral actions such as trying on a bathing suit by oneself increased a woman's body shame. "Anything that primes a woman to focus on her body shape," Engeln concluded, "is much more likely to . . . leave her feeling dissatisfied with her appearance."[6]

However, US culture also promotes harsh beauty standards to boys and men. Boys and men face pressure to be lean and thin. A 2014 study of teen boys in the United States found that almost 20 percent were worried about their weight and body shape.[7] Male beauty standards also favor tall men over shorter ones. Boys and men face additional pressure to have toned bodies with visible muscles. Many male action heroes and superheroes in popular media tend to be unusually muscular. Most people cannot achieve these types of muscles, since each body gains muscle differently. In fact, many Hollywood actors have to use steroids for the ultramuscular look. These drugs increase the body's natural ability to build muscle. However, they also have many negative side effects, including mood swings, increased risk of heart attack, and high blood pressure. According to a 2019 study published in the *International Journal of Eating Disorders*, over 20 percent of teen boys and young adult men had what they called "muscularity-oriented disordered eating."[8] In other words, they used unhealthy habits, such as following a heavily restricted diet, in order to help build muscle.

BODY IMAGE AND RACE

Since beauty standards are often symbols of status and power, they help some groups of people claim unfair advantages. The United States has a long history of racial inequality and oppression, with white people claiming disproportionate political, financial, and social power. As a result, many US beauty standards favor traits that are associated with whiteness, such as pale skin. This association has often been maintained through rules and policies. For example, until 1940, only white women could compete in the

GENDER DYSPHORIA

Someone who is transgender (trans) identifies as a gender other than the one assigned at birth. They may identify as another gender, genderqueer, agender, or nonbinary. Some trans people experience gender dysphoria, which is the distress caused by having a gender identity that does not match the sex assigned at birth. Often, people can alleviate symptoms of gender dysphoria by presenting themselves in ways that match their gender identities. Gender presentation is the collection of outward signs that communicate gender or a lack of gender.

Puberty and the teen years are a common time for trans teens to feel gender dysphoria. The physical changes of puberty, as well as the development of secondary sex characteristics such as breasts and body hair, may make transgender teens begin to feel that their bodies do not match their selves. Trans teens may also feel pressure to present their genders as either hypermasculine or hyperfeminine in order for society to accept their gender identities.

SKIN TONE AND BEAUTY STANDARDS

US beauty standards on skin color are contradictory. On the one hand, racist beauty standards favor lighter-skinned people over darker-skinned people. Darker-skinned models, for example, report being passed over in favor of lighter-skinned colleagues, and dark-skinned actors talk about having trouble getting roles. On the other hand, many light-skinned people would like to have darker skin and use lotions and tanning beds to achieve this look. However, it can be problematic for white people to purposely darken their skin. Celebrities such as Kim Kardashian and Ariana Grande face criticism for consistently tanning their skin darker than its natural color. Skin darkening, critics explain, can be seen as a form of cultural appropriation, where people imitate the looks or behaviors of people from another culture without truly understanding and respecting their origins.

Miss America pageant. Today, media and advertising strengthen the false impression that white beauty standards are universal. Many commercials, for instance, feature white actors and models. As of 2019, about 40 percent of the US population identified as Black, Hispanic, Asian, Native or Pacific Islander, or multiracial.[9] According to the University of California, Los Angeles's 2019 Hollywood Diversity Report, however, only about 20 percent of lead actors in movies and TV shows were people of color.[10]

Racialized beauty standards can also be tools of discrimination.

Black Americans are often told that their natural hair textures or hair styles are "unprofessional" or "out of control" because of white, European-based beauty standards.

In 2017, Jenesis Johnson, a Black teenager at North Florida Christian School, wore her natural hair in a rounded shape known as an Afro. One day, her teacher stopped instruction to ask Johnson when she would be changing her hair. Other students began to ask similar questions. Later that week, the school's assistant principal told Johnson her natural hair was "out of control."[11] The school administration told

Johnson that if she did not change her hair, she could not attend the school the following semester.

According to school rules, students could not wear hairstyles that were "extreme" or trendy. But the Afro hairstyle is not extreme, as Johnson and her family pointed out. In fact, Johnson had been wearing her hair that way for years. Johnson's mother noted that the school sent the message that curly, kinky hair was considered less acceptable than other types of natural hair. Across the country, Black students and employees report similar stories. They recall being told their natural hair was inappropriate or unclean, or that they needed to change their appearances for reasons that seemed baseless and discriminatory. By 2019, seven states had proposed or enacted laws designed to fight this specific form of discrimination.[12]

Racist beauty standards place an extra burden on people of color, even when teens do not internalize, or come to agree with, the messages those standards send. Some Black people grow up hearing they should use chemical relaxers on their hair in order to make it more similar to non-Black hair, but these relaxers can be dangerous and can permanently damage a person's hair. Johnson's mother makes a point of telling her daughter she is beautiful the way she is, and specifically that her hair is beautiful in its natural state.

TECHNOLOGY AND BODY IMAGE

The social media landscape for teens has changed drastically in the past decade. By the end of 2019, approximately 70 percent of teens used the social media apps Instagram and Snapchat.[13] For teens, the pressure to look good on social media can increase self-consciousness and decrease confidence. A 2018 study found that, for teens, posting a lot of photos on social media was related to feeling more negatively toward their bodies.

Social media apps also play a role in promoting beauty standards. Instagram and Snapchat both offer filters that play with color and perception to change the look of a photo. Some of these filters warp a person's facial features, often to fit certain beauty standards. For example, the Snapchat "pretty" filter enlarges the appearance of the user's eyes, thins out the cheeks and nose, and smooths the appearance of skin.

> "WE CAN LIVE IN A WORLD WHERE WE TRY TO DO BATTLE WITH THOSE OVERARCHING NARRATIVES. BUT THE FORCES PUSHING BACK AGAINST IT IN MANY PARTS OF THE WORLD—IT'S QUITE A HEADWIND."[14]
>
> —NOLIWE ROOKS, PROFESSOR AND RESEARCHER ON RACE AND BEAUTY

The filter defines these features as "pretty," implying that other types of facial features are not pretty.

While some social media filters change a person's hair color or create sparkles in the background, others change the shape of a person's face to make it fit in with society's beauty standards.

Social media can also be a tool for bullying and body shaming. According to a 2018 Pew Research study, almost 60 percent of teens had been cyberbullied in some way.[15] High schooler Chloe remembers seeing a body-shaming comment on the private Instagram account of a girl she knew. "It started this whole big thing," Chloe told *Allure* magazine. "It hurt a lot of . . . my own friends' feelings."[16]

Teens who are trying to form a healthy body image face many challenges at the same time. Society sends restrictive and harmful messages about which types of bodies are most valuable. Social media and peer networks help reinforce these messages. When teens internalize beauty standards and promote them through their relationships and social media, they can help promote inequalities and poor body image as well.

Teens with BDD may feel compelled to assess their bodies in a mirror multiple times per day.

CHAPTER FOUR

BODY DYSMORPHIC DISORDER

For some teens, negative body image goes beyond occasional or moderate feelings of body dissatisfaction. For people with BDD, negative body image becomes so severe that it is difficult or impossible to live a normal life. People with BDD suffer from ongoing negative thoughts and feelings about their bodies or about certain parts of their bodies. These thoughts and mindsets feel as though they are outside a person's control. Between 2 and 3 percent of people in the United States suffer from BDD, and women are slightly more likely than men to have a BDD diagnosis. Most people with BDD start showing symptoms by age 18, and it is most common for symptoms to begin around 12 or 13.[1]

BDD can come in many forms. Some BDD sufferers may feel unhappy with their appearance as a whole, believing that they are too fat, not muscular enough, or just generally unattractive. Others focus on a specific body part, such as a facial feature or blemish. Nicole, who

OLFACTORY REFERENCE SYNDROME

Olfactory Reference Syndrome (ORS) is a disorder in which people are severely distressed by their bodies' real or imagined smells. Some researchers consider ORS a type of BDD, while others think of it as a separate but very similar disorder. Like people with BDD, ORS sufferers have obsessive thoughts about the way they smell and engage in repetitive behaviors. These behaviors can include showering too often or putting on lots of perfume. People with ORS usually smell completely normal to others, and like BDD, ORS is so distressing that it makes living a normal life difficult.

has BDD, shared her story with the BDD Foundation. She stated, "I remember when I was only nine years old I thought about cutting off my nose because it was too big."[2] She started wearing a jacket to school so she could cover her face with its sleeves. Eventually, Nicole's BDD became so severe that she started to critique and hate other parts of her appearance. She also suffered from disordered eating and addiction.

CRITERIA FOR BDD

The diagnosis, or official identification, of BDD is made by health-care professionals. Specialists in mental health, such as psychiatrists and clinical psychologists, diagnose BDD. In the United States, a manual called the *Diagnostic and Statistical Manual of Mental Disorders*, or *DSM*, gives guidelines on how to recognize psychological disorders, such as BDD, in patients. The latest edition is the *DSM-5*, which was published in 2013. It defines four main aspects of the disorder. People with BDD feel distress and concern about some parts of how they look, but other people do not notice these perceived flaws or do not perceive the individual with BDD to have any appearance flaws. People with BDD also have repetitive physical or mental behaviors that they cannot control. For example, people with BDD often "mirror-check," or look at themselves over and over again in the mirror. They may also pick at their skin, moles, or pimples. Some people may find themselves unable to stop ruminating about their bodies, returning to the same negative thoughts over and over again.

According to the *DSM-5*, these negative thoughts, feelings, and behaviors cause "clinically significant distress," or are bad enough that they make it difficult for the person to carry on with important parts of life.[3] Patients who are mostly concerned with their bodies in relation to food and eating should not be diagnosed with BDD. Additionally, people who are not diagnosed with BDD but have negative body image may also experience symptoms of depression and anxiety.

People with BDD also have different levels of insight into their situation. Some BDD sufferers—those with good to fair insight—have some level of awareness that they

Health-care providers and mental health professionals can diagnose patients with BDD. They can also refer patients to experts for more specialized treatment.

look normal to other people, even though they cannot stop thinking about their perceived flaws. However, other people do not have this ability, and they believe that others see them the way they see themselves.

WHAT CAUSES BDD?

People who research BDD believe that the causes of this disorder are biopsychosocial. This means that biological, psychological, and social factors influence someone developing BDD. Biological factors include inherited characteristics. Some people may be predisposed to develop BDD based on their genetics.

Psychological factors may also contribute to BDD. For example, one study found signs of differences between the brains of people with BDD and those of people without the illness. When researchers had study participants look at photos of people's faces, people with BDD were more likely to focus on specific facial features and details. People without BDD were more likely to look at the face as a whole. Researchers think that people who have the ability to notice and focus on small visual details may be more vulnerable to BDD because small flaws or inconsistencies stick out in their minds.

THE HISTORY OF BDD

BDD was first diagnosed in the late 1800s by an Italian doctor named Enrico Morselli. He called the illness *dysmorphophobia*. Other European doctors found and diagnosed patients with BDD in the early 1900s. They treated the illness using early forms of talk therapy. In 1987, body dysmorphic disorder was added to the *DSM* for the first time. And in 2013, the *DSM-5* classified BDD as an obsessive-compulsive and related disorder.

Social factors are the influences of environment and upbringing, or the ways that family, friends, personal experiences, and society at large shape who we are. People who experience abuse as children, including

bullying, are more likely to suffer from BDD. A 2017 study in *Body Image* found that many BDD patients say that childhood or adolescent bullying directly contributed to their disorder. And the social messaging that all people receive about beauty standards, whether within families and communities or from the media, plays a role in the development of people's body image and informs the way they feel about how they look.

Biological, psychological, and social factors affect each other. A person's biology helps shape the way they think and feel, and personality and thinking patterns make a huge difference in how people perceive and react in different social situations. The roots of BDD may vary from person to person, but there are some tendencies, thoughts, and experiences that people with the illness are more likely to share with each other.

LIFE WITH BDD

Life with BDD can be isolating and limited. One common thread in stories of people with BDD is a sense that the illness disconnects them from other

Some people with BDD report that they experienced abuse or bullying as children.

BDD BY PROXY

Some people experience BDD by proxy, finding themselves unable to stop fixating on another person's body or appearance. A 2013 study in the journal *Body Image* looked at the symptoms and experiences of 11 people with BDD by proxy. As a whole, the patients with BDD by proxy had symptoms very similar to those of other BDD patients. They spent hours thinking about perceived physical flaws and had rituals in place to help correct them. However, the people whose appearances they worried about varied greatly. They worried about family members and strangers and had an average of five people each whose appearance distressed them.[4]

> "I PICKED MY SKIN UNTIL I GAVE MYSELF SCARS, THEN I STAYED IN MY ROOM TO PICK AT THE SCARS RATHER THAN GO OUTSIDE THE HOUSE WITH FAMILY OR FRIENDS."[5]
>
> —MATT, *BDD SUFFERER*

people and from the lives they want to live. Jesa Marie Calaor wrote about her experience with BDD in an essay for *Allure* magazine. Calaor is small, thin, and athletic, and she became consumed with the feeling that she wasn't small or toned enough. Calaor finally realized that her preoccupation with exercise and appearance was tiring her out and making it impossible to concentrate. She accepted a doctor's suggestion that she might have BDD and sought treatment.

People with more severe cases of BDD may find themselves unable to keep up

Some people with BDD are so preoccupied with their perceived flaws that they feel anxious or depressed when they try to leave the house.

responsibilities such as going to school or keeping a job. Some BDD sufferers become completely housebound. Their fear of being seen by others is so strong that they avoid contact with other people entirely. Paul developed BDD at age 15, feeling self-conscious about his pale skin. "At one stage," he wrote in a blog entry, "I didn't leave the house for nearly 2 years."[6]

BDD is a life-threatening illness. People with BDD are at an especially high risk of suicidal thoughts and behaviors. People who begin suffering from BDD as teens are even more likely to consider or attempt suicide. But there is hope. People with BDD tend to respond well to effective mental health treatment.

One symptom of depression is low energy that makes it difficult to complete everyday tasks.

CHAPTER FIVE

BDD AND OTHER CONDITIONS

When two diseases or disorders occur together, they are called comorbid. BDD is frequently comorbid with several other mental disorders, including major depressive disorder, substance abuse disorders, obsessive-compulsive disorders, and social anxiety disorder. The relationship between two or more comorbid disorders is often very complex. One disorder may play a role in causing the other, or the two may have the same root cause. In some cases, it's not known exactly why two disorders tend to be found together. People who have negative body image but do not fit the criteria for BDD are also at higher risk of depression and anxiety. Teens who suffer from body image issues should also be aware of the signs and symptoms of other mental disorders.

MAJOR DEPRESSIVE DISORDER AND BDD

Major depressive disorder, or depression, is a mental disorder that causes persistent low mood and sadness.

People with depression often suffer from a lack of energy, as well as sleep and eating disturbances. Depression tends to affect the ability to concentrate and think. Depressed people may suffer from a brain fog, where they cannot focus, or they may feel stuck ruminating on negative thoughts. People with depression may also suffer from constant feelings of guilt, even though they've done nothing wrong.

The strongest defining features of depression are low mood and low energy. Depression may also make it difficult for people to complete daily tasks such as showering and cooking meals. This suggests, but does not prove, that the challenges of life with BDD may make developing depression more likely. According to the BDD Foundation, many BDD sufferers feel as if life with BDD is the largest contributor to their depression, and that they would not consider themselves clinically depressed if they were not dealing with BDD symptoms.

SOCIAL ANXIETY DISORDER AND BDD

Social anxiety disorder is a mental disorder in which people feel significant anxiety about interacting with others. It is also known as social phobia. Social anxiety disorder and BDD have key features in common. People who have either illness are very concerned about being seen, evaluated, and judged by others.

For people with BDD, this anxiety centers around their hated body part, whereas social anxiety sufferers are typically more concerned with people's opinions of their actions and behaviors. Both social anxiety disorder patients and BDD patients may stay home to avoid having to be around other people. Social anxiety disorder can be a contributor to BDD, and people who have both disorders usually suffer from social anxiety disorder first.

LOW SELF-ESTEEM

Self-esteem is a feeling of confidence in one's worth and abilities. People with high self-esteem generally think well of themselves, and people with low self-esteem struggle to feel that they are worth treating with respect. Self-esteem and body image are deeply linked. Negative body image can contribute to low self-esteem, and the reverse is also true. Low self-esteem, in turn, is a risk factor for poor mental health and conditions such as substance abuse, anxiety, and depression.

Crowded public places, including transportation like buses and subways, can be stressful for people with social anxiety.

OBSESSIVE-COMPULSIVE DISORDER AND BDD

The *DSM-5* classifies BDD among obsessive-compulsive and related disorders. Obsessions are thoughts that a person can't control or limit, and compulsions are repeated behaviors that people engage in to try to suppress or neutralize their obsessions. Obsessive-compulsive disorder (OCD) is the most well-known of these disorders.

People with OCD have obsessive thoughts that cause them a great deal of distress. They engage in compulsive behaviors to try to reduce distress brought about by their obsession. Like BDD symptoms, OCD symptoms take up significant time in the sufferer's day, cause significant pain and anxiety, and make it difficult to live daily life. Patients who have both BDD and OCD will demonstrate specific body-related obsessions and compulsions. However, people with OCD also have compulsive behaviors that are not related to appearance.

BODY IMAGE WORLDWIDE

In 2015, the research firm YouGov carried out a study of body image in adults in 25 countries worldwide. It polled people in 13 countries in Asia and the Middle East, seven countries in Europe, four in the Americas, and Australia. YouGov found that the country with the highest average body-positive feelings was Indonesia, followed by Saudi Arabia, Oman, and Qatar. Hong Kong had the lowest average body image, and the United States was fifth from lowest. Two trends tended to hold true across cultures. Men tended to have higher body image than women, and body image improved with age.[2]

SUBSTANCE USE DISORDER AND BDD

Some people with BDD try to relieve their symptoms with substances such as alcohol or other drugs. These substances can temporarily ease anxiety and give a pleasurable, relaxed feeling. However, only drugs prescribed by a mental health professional have a good chance of truly relieving BDD symptoms in the long term. If BDD sufferers grow dependent on drugs or alcohol for symptom management, they can develop a substance use disorder.

The *DSM-5* classifies a substance use disorder as occurring when substance use becomes significantly harmful and outside the user's control. Substance use disorders range from mild or moderate to severe, but substance use disorders have a significant negative effect on daily life no matter the severity. Substance abuse can also change the way the brain works. Substance use of any kind is most common in older teens and young adults, and substance abuse in the teen years can make the symptoms of BDD worse. About half of all people with BDD also have a substance use disorder at some point in their lives. Alcohol is the most common substance abused by people with BDD.

EATING DISORDERS AND BDD

Eating disorders are a cluster of disorders whose main symptoms are unhealthy, harmful patterns of eating. People with eating disorders may compulsively undereat, may overeat, or may lose control over their eating. They may also purge their food through vomiting or taking

People with eating disorders may have a perception of their body size that differs from reality. In the above photo, a woman with anorexia compares her perception of her waist size (the red rope) with an actual measurement of her waist size (the blue rope).

laxatives, even though these actions are dangerous and ineffective. The symptoms of many eating disorders overlap with those of BDD. This is especially true for BDD patients who focus on their weight and overall body type. They may check themselves obsessively and change their lifestyles because of their mental illness. Patients can suffer from both BDD and an eating disorder. This might be especially likely to occur in patients who are preoccupied

HELP FOR EATING DISORDERS

Eating disorders can be severe and sometimes fatal to their sufferers. Just as negative body image is very common in US culture, unhealthy patterns of eating can sometimes seem normal, accepted, or even glamorized. The National Eating Disorders Association (NEDA) offers information and help to people with eating disorders and their loved ones. The organization's website, nationaleatingdisorders.org, helps explain what eating disorders are and offers a screening tool. The tool asks questions designed to help people decide whether they may have an eating disorder. NEDA also points people in the direction of local resources such as therapists and treatment centers. Its helpline is accessible by phone at 1-800-931-2237, and it also offers an online chat function and crisis text service.

with their weight and size as well as with another body feature.

Individuals whose BDD involves weight and muscularity fixations are also at risk of orthorexia. Orthorexia is a pattern of disordered eating centered around the perception of healthy eating. People with orthorexia become fixated on eating healthfully or having a "correct" or "clean" diet to the point that their behavior actually becomes unhealthy. For example, a person with orthorexia might cut out all food groups she thinks are bad for her, such as sugar, all carbs, and animal fats. This leaves her with few choices of what to eat on a daily basis, and puts her at risk of nutritional deficits, especially when paired with excessive exercise. Orthorexia is not recognized as an eating disorder by the *DSM-5*. However, many health-care professionals and organizations such as the National Eating Disorders Association (NEDA) recognize it.

Disordered eating does not always relate to someone's body image. Many people with eating disorders describe using their eating behaviors to change not just how they look but also how they feel. For example, patients with anorexia nervosa, an eating disorder that usually includes extreme, unhealthy weight loss, often describe restricted eating as a way to feel in control. Other people with Avoidant Restrictive Food Intake Disorder (ARFID) may severely restrict the types of foods they eat based on the texture, temperature, or other sensory characteristics of the food. Those with eating disorders may struggle with symptoms even when they are content with the way their bodies look, although this applies to a minority of people with eating disorders. Because BDD and eating disorders often have different causes but share certain symptoms, it's important to diagnosis them correctly.

Teens with unhealthy body image may wear multiple layers of clothing to disguise the size and shape of their bodies.

CHAPTER SIX

THE EFFECTS OF UNHEALTHY BODY IMAGE

People cope with feelings about their bodies in different ways. There are small everyday strategies that can help soothe body image anxiety. A person with negative feelings about a birthmark might cover it up with clothing, or a person who worries about how they look might say positive things in the mirror before going out in public. People with unhealthy body image also report feeling like they can't live life to the fullest. They may miss out on opportunities because their negative feelings keep them isolated and unsure.

BODY IMAGE, UNDEREATING, AND CRASH DIETING

Many people deal with negative feelings about weight by dieting or undereating. Undereating can be chronic, or it can be short-term in the form of crash diets. While undereating is harmful for anyone, it is especially harmful for people whose bodies are still developing.

CLEANSES AND CRASH DIETING

Magazines and websites sometimes promote "healthy" eating in the form of cleanses, which are short-term restrictive diets meant to improve health. Cleanses sometimes promise that they can radically change the body's appearance in a short amount of time. However, the average cleanse is just a crash diet in disguise. For example, a famous diet called the Master Cleanse tells dieters to eat or drink nothing but salt water, spiced lemonade, or a special tea. The creator of the cleanse claims this heavily restricted diet "detoxifies" the system. However, cleanses like this one deprive the body of necessary nutrients. The drastic weight loss that people experience is not only a loss of fat but also muscle, bone, and water. The word *cleanse* is a misnomer. It suggests that these diets do something to detoxify the body. However, the body has natural processes to remove toxins in the liver and kidneys. There is no medical evidence that cleanses help the body purify itself, and, in fact, they can be dangerous.

When the body does not get enough calories to function properly, the person may have difficulty concentrating or staying alert. Malnutrition also negatively affects bone development, skin, and hair, and it can cause people to have difficulty performing daily physical tasks.

In the long term, undereating can be very dangerous. Mary Cain was a teenager who excelled at distance running, a sport she loved. By age 17, she was the youngest US runner to ever join a team that competed in the track and field World Championships. In her freshman year of

Mary Cain, *center*, felt pressured by her coaches to change the way her body looked in order to continue competing at the top level.

college, Cain accepted a sponsorship from Nike to train with a well-known coach and team of champion athletes. She thought she was on the way to achieving her dream. Instead, her coach and staff constantly pressured her to lose weight and to keep losing it. Cain internalized this standard and became preoccupied with her weight.

The coaches' focus on Cain's weight had a devastating effect on her body. She developed a syndrome called RED-S, or relative energy deficiency in sports. Athletes with this syndrome do not take in enough calories to meet their bodies' energy needs and can suffer from lower bone density and altered hormones. Cain did not menstruate for three years. Her lack of estrogen, a necessary hormone, weakened her bones, and she suffered five different bone fractures. Cain's running suffered, and so did her mental health. She began to self-harm. Eventually, Cain quit the team for her own survival. Cain has seen other women athletes suffer as a result of their coaches' unhealthy and abusive focus on weight. "Young girls' bodies are being ruined by an emotionally and physically abusive system," she told the *New York Times*.[1]

> "AMONG MY FRIENDS, THEIR BIGGEST INSECURITY IS PROBABLY . . . WHAT THEIR BODY LOOKS LIKE."[2]
>
> —*SAVANNAH, TEENAGER*

BODY IMAGE, SELF-ESTEEM, AND SOCIAL LIFE

Unhealthy body image can dampen confidence and self-esteem in all areas of life. In 2017, the company Dove, which sells personal-care products such as soap and lotion, funded a study on the body confidence of girls ages ten to 17 across the world. The researchers interviewed more than 5,000 girls in 14 countries, including the United States. They found that 80 percent of girls with poor body image would skip extracurriculars or stop spending time with friends if they didn't like how they looked.[3] This was true even though most of the girls interviewed were critical of the beauty standards they'd been taught.

Seventy percent of the girls in the study said that the societies in which they lived made

BODY IMAGE AND WOMEN'S SPORTS

For women athletes, body image can be incredibly difficult to navigate. Regular exercise can be a huge body image boost. Some studies show that female athletes tend to have better body image than those who don't play sports. But the demands of some sports are at odds with female beauty standards that ask women to be small and thin. Some teen and young adult athletes worry about putting on muscle, or "getting big," as a result of heavy training. Others, like Mary Cain, are pressured to keep their weight low while competing at their sport.

beauty seem very important. The girls also supported diverse beauty standards. They were savvy about the harmful messages that media and culture fed them.[4] But being aware of beauty myths does not always cancel out their negative effects.

THE RISKS OF OVEREXERCISING

Some teens with negative body image may exercise to excess. Exercise can be a BDD repetitive behavior that is used to deal with obsessive concerns about body shape. People with muscle dysmorphia, for example, are likely to overexercise. Overexercise, or compulsive exercise, can lead to a decrease in athletic performance when the body is deprived of needed rest. It can cause tiredness and insomnia. Compulsive exercise also increases the risk of injury, especially since some overexercisers will continue to train despite being hurt. In addition, compulsive exercise takes away time from other activities, such as work, school, and time with friends.

Like many studies of teens and body image, the Dove study focused on teen girls only. Other perspectives were not included. Future research can investigate how boys and nonbinary teens react to similar appearance pressures.

People with unhealthy body image may hold themselves back from pursuing the things they want in life. They are also at risk for settling for less in their relationships. According to a 2016 article in the journal *Body Image*, people who were unhappy with their weight and appearance were more likely to be unhappy with life in general. The study found that people who didn't like the way they looked were more likely to worry that romantic partners would leave them.

When people dislike their bodies and themselves, it can feel natural to be surrounded by other people who reinforce their negative self-image. They may feel like they don't deserve friends who love them for who they are, or even that no one is capable of accepting the way they look. Patrick Ferris remembers the person he was in middle and high school. He felt uncomfortable in his own skin, despising the chubby stomach he now enjoys and appreciates. He put up with close friends who told him his body made him less attractive. It took therapy and improvement in his body image for him to start seeking out better friends. After therapy, "I . . . saw that being friends with people who viewed me as lesser because of my body was not obligatory, but optional," Ferris wrote in an essay for *Rookie* magazine.[5]

THE PRESSURE TO BE BEAUTIFUL

Many people form thoughts and opinions about others based on personal appearance. People use personal style and nonverbal gestures such as smiles to send messages about who they are. It's natural to pick up on these messages, learning about people through their presentation and body language. But judging a book by its cover can only go so far. People are more than what they look like. Even for people who do fit societal beauty standards, the pressure to maintain a body that other people approve of can be exhausting.

The practice of treating a person like a collection of body parts instead of a human being is called objectification. Objectification can feel disrespectful or hostile. Many girls and women report feeling objectified by others. For example, a man who stares rudely at the breasts of a woman nearby, not caring whether he is making her uncomfortable, is sexually objectifying her. Some people internalize this attitude toward their bodies and objectify themselves. When people self-objectify, they think of their own bodies in terms of what they think other people find sexy or appealing.

Because girls and women feel more of the effects of society's beauty standards than boys and men do, self-objectification is more common in girls than in boys. However, some men do self-objectify. Self-objectification is harmful to body image. A 2017 research review in *Frontiers in Psychology* noted that self-objectification often leads to more self-consciousness and shame about appearance. This shame exists even in people who are well aware that they are considered sexy or beautiful.

Self-objectification makes feeling comfortable in your own body very difficult, even when you manage to meet beauty standards. Siera Bearchell grew up with an easy relationship with her body. She liked dancing and staying

One form of objectification is catcalling, or street harassment. Many women report being approached by strangers who make comments about their bodies.

active, ate what she wanted, and didn't pay attention to what other people said about her body. When she was a teen, she got involved in beauty pageants, thinking that they could offer her a way to volunteer and travel. Bearchell succeeded in the pageant circuit. By the time she was 20, Bearchell placed second in the Miss Universe pageant in her native Canada. She was told that she would need to get thinner in order to make it further in her career.

While Siera Bearchell did not win the Miss Universe pageant in 2016, she competed in a way that felt authentic and true to her healthy body image.

Even though she had never been unhappy with her weight, Bearchell started dieting so drastically that she didn't have the energy to study or work out. She found herself obsessively comparing herself to the other beautiful women she competed with. "I was told 'If you want to be successful, this is what you have to do,' and no matter how strong of a person you are, it's really easy to fall under that pressure," Bearchell said.[6]

Eventually, Bearchell decided that she needed to compete as the person she really was. She won Miss Universe Canada 2016 and competed in the world Miss Universe pageant with a body that was larger than those of most of the contestants. Today, Bearchell has a law degree and works as a model, body image activist, and pageant coach. She uses her social media to remind herself and others that they can be their own judges of their bodies' beauty and worth.

OBJECTIFICATION IN MIDDLE SCHOOL AND HIGH SCHOOL

Many girls experience sexual objectification from other students, as well as from staff and teachers during the course of the school day. These experiences of objectification can have lasting harmful effects. Research suggests that the feeling of being objectified can make women perform worse on academic tasks like math tests. Some girls are fighting back against sexual objectification inside their schools. In 2019, for example, a group of high schoolers in Maryland found a list that ranked girls' looks on a point scale. Dozens of the girls on the list got together to confront the list maker and the administration. The boy who made the list apologized and began participating in weekly conversations on body image.

Some teens with negative body image may find it helpful to attend group therapy sessions or participate in support groups.

CHAPTER SEVEN

TREATMENT OPTIONS

Negative body image is so widespread among teens that it is, to a certain extent, a normal part of daily teen life. And teens who suffer from poor body image may feel like there is no one who can understand and help them with their symptoms. However, talk therapy and medication are both effective treatments for BDD, and talk therapy is an effective treatment for negative body image.

People living with BDD have a variety of therapy options to choose from, and some therapists blend approaches. Medication can ease symptoms, making it easier for people with BDD to meet everyday challenges. For teens who do not have BDD but want to work toward a better body image, a healthy, accepting lifestyle can have huge mental health benefits.

TREATMENT FOR UNHEALTHY BODY IMAGE OR BDD

For people who think they might have BDD, it can be hard to know what to do next. Before treatment can begin, BDD must be diagnosed by a health-care professional. Doctors, some nurses, and licensed therapists are trained to make

COSMETIC SURGERY AND BDD

Patients with BDD usually try to get cosmetic surgery, or plastic surgery, to help fix their perceived flaws. However, even when a cosmetic surgery is successful, BDD sufferers are more likely than others to be disappointed with its results.

BDD causes its sufferers to incorrectly perceive how their "flaws" look to themselves and others. Cosmetic surgery cannot fix this problem of skewed perception. For this reason, a majority of cosmetic surgeons report that they will not perform surgery on a patient they believe has BDD. However, cosmetic surgeons may not be screening their patients well enough for signs of BDD. A 2016 survey of American Society for Aesthetic Plastic Surgery members found that the vast majority had operated on a BDD patient without knowing it at the time.[1]

these diagnoses. A primary care doctor or health-care professional is a good first resource for a teen with BDD symptoms. During an appointment, a health-care provider can discuss symptoms of BDD with a patient. The doctor might be ready to make a BDD diagnosis or might decide to get the opinion of another professional. Either way, the next step would be for the doctor to make a referral.

Primary care doctors and pediatricians can refer patients to local mental health specialists such as psychiatrists, clinical psychologists, and licensed social workers.

These professionals can begin talk therapy treatments, often in weekly in-person sessions of 30 minutes to an hour. Psychiatrists, who are medical doctors who focus on mental disorders, can also prescribe medication. In some cases, BDD patients work with a psychiatrist and a therapist, or with a team of professionals. For instance, a person with BDD might see a clinical psychologist for therapy sessions and a psychiatrist for help managing prescription medications.

However, it's possible to not have a diagnosis of BDD and still feel that an unhealthy body image is making life difficult. Talk therapists often work with patients who do not have BDD but struggle with body image, and they are available to help anyone who is suffering from negative body thoughts and feelings.

THERAPY OPTIONS

Talk therapists use a variety of approaches to help patients who struggle with body image. One that has been demonstrated to help many individuals with BDD is cognitive behavioral therapy, or CBT. In CBT, patients work to understand the deeper thoughts and beliefs that drive their actions. Then, they work to change those beliefs by making manageable changes to their daily actions. CBT therapists use thoughtful questions to help guide patients to an understanding of their core beliefs. Then, they help patients consider whether these beliefs are true or helpful. For example, a person who believes that no one can stand to look at her hair might have a deeply rooted belief that she is unlovable the way she is. Once the patient has identified some harmful beliefs, she can work to change them.

CBT therapists often give their patients homework aimed at helping them practice healthier thoughts and behaviors. For example, a cognitive behavioral worksheet might ask a patient about something they worry might happen to their appearance. Then, the worksheet would ask them to describe how likely the event is to actually happen, the worst-case scenario if it did happen, and how they would cope if it did happen. This worksheet could help patients from catastrophizing, or imagining extremely negative outcomes to average situations.

Therapists might also work with their clients through exposure therapy, which helps them gradually confront their body-related fears. Therapists might ask patients to rate the things they are afraid of on a scale from least to most scary. For instance, a BDD patient who hates his acne

Psychiatrists can work with people who are living with BDD. They may prescribe medications to help with anxiety and depression associated with BDD.

scars might find it a little scary to hang out with a family member while not wearing makeup. However, meeting up with a friend without makeup might feel scarier, and giving a presentation in front of other people might seem terrifying. With the therapist's help, the patient starts facing those fears, starting at the least scary end of the scale and working upward.

ACCEPTANCE AND COMMITMENT THERAPY

Acceptance and commitment therapy (ACT) is another talk therapy approach sometimes used for BDD patients. ACT is based on the idea that it is possible to welcome negative emotions and distressing thoughts without acting on them or avoiding them. In one study, published in the journal *Behavior Therapy* in 2015, 21 BDD patients underwent a 12-week group ACT program that included education about their condition, practice in ACT techniques, and different types of exposure. These treatments were designed to "foster acceptance of internal discomfort and to strengthen the patients' committed purposeful actions." At the end of the study, 68 percent of participants showed "clinically significant improvement," which was maintained by participants through a follow-up appointment that occurred six months after the study concluded.[3] Through ACT, it may be possible for BDD patients to discover their true values and work to live them out day to day, even though they may experience distress.

MEDICATION OPTIONS

People with diagnosed mental disorders may choose to take medication to help manage their symptoms. The most common types of medications prescribed for people with BDD, as well as comorbid disorders like depression, anxiety, and OCD, are called selective serotonin reuptake inhibitors (SSRIs). SSRIs work by making more of the neurotransmitter serotonin available. Serotonin is a chemical that sends messages between neurons. It is believed that serotonin helps lift mood. Researchers believe that having more serotonin

SSRIs, depicted here in pink, block serotonin, shown as the orange spheres, from reentering neurons. This increases the amount of available serotonin in the brain.

available in the brain can help combat the symptoms of depression and anxiety. These medications can also help ease symptoms of BDD. According to the International OCD Foundation, SSRIs significantly reduce symptoms in about two-thirds of BDD patients.[4] The medications don't change what patients choose to think about, but they can have a calming effect that makes obsessive thoughts less frequent or less intrusive. Although SSRIs are generally safe, they can have side effects such as

The HAES movement stresses the importance of health and fitness for people rather than body size or appearance.

insomnia or appetite changes and can increase thoughts of suicide. Medications should be used under the guidance of a doctor.

BODY IMAGE AND LIFESTYLE

Exercise and healthy eating are good for physical health, and they're known to elevate mood. Doctors often recommend exercise for people who suffer from depression and anxiety. But for people who struggle with anxiety around weight and size, it can be tempting to focus too much on diets and workouts. Some people enjoy pushing their physical limits or spending their free time crafting healthy meals. But exercise doesn't have to be strenuous to help change body image. According to a 2017 study by health and exercise science professor Kathleen Martin Ginis, just one moderate bout of 30 minute exercise can help young women improve their body image.[5] Additionally, yoga, a low-impact exercise that focuses on physical and mental well-being, has been demonstrated to help improve young women's body image.

Size diversity is the idea that people naturally come in different shapes and sizes, which should be celebrated. The Association for Size Diversity and Health (ASDAH) created the Health at Every Size moment, or HAES. HAES advocates an approach to health that isn't related to body size. According to the organization's website, the approach "promotes balanced

> "ONE OF MY MOST SIGNIFICANT REALIZATIONS IS THAT CHANGING MY BODY DOES NOT MEAN I WILL AUTOMATICALLY LOVE MYSELF. I HAVE LEARNED THAT SELF-LOVE AND BODY IMAGE HAVE FAR MORE TO DO WITH MY MENTAL STATE THAN MY PHYSICAL APPEARANCE."[7]
> —EMILY LOCKE, BLOGGER

eating, life-enhancing physical activity, and respect for the diversity of body shapes and sizes."[6] As plus-size fitness trainer and HAES advocate Louise Green points out, many people may have early negative experiences with fitness and exercise. They may remember gym classes where they were made fun of or pushed past their limits. HAES, according to Green, "asks people to revisit fitness in a joyful way."[8]

DERMATOLOGY AND BDD

BDD patients usually seek help with their physical appearance long before they decide to get mental health treatment. They will often go to dermatologists, or doctors specializing in skin, to get help with skin problems that never seem to truly improve. According to the BDD Foundation, "Research shows that most individuals with [BDD] have been seeing a dermatologist for almost 10 years before they finally visit a therapist."[9] Because BDD patients so often turn to dermatologists, dermatologist Elizabeth Damstetter recommends screening all patients for signs of BDD. Damstetter tells colleagues to look out for patients who have seemingly invisible flaws or who want to copy the looks of celebrities.

HELPING OTHERS WITH POOR BODY IMAGE

The path to mental illness recovery can be long, with unexpected twists and turns. After a period of treatment and recovery, a person with poor body image or BDD may experience a lapse, or temporary, milder return of symptoms. There's also the possibility of relapse. If a relapse happens, it's no reason for self-blame or despair. Body image experts encourage patients to monitor themselves for symptoms and reach out for extra support at the sign of a lapse. They also work with their patients during treatment to plan ahead for the possibility of lapses. By committing to good self-care and continued treatment, teens can reduce anxiety by thinking ahead about challenging future situations, such as dating or wearing new kinds of clothing, and planning how they'd like to react.

It can be hard to see a friend or loved one suffer from BDD or unhealthy body image. Knowing that someone you love can't love and accept themselves is

RESPONDING TO NEGATIVE SELF-TALK

When loved ones or friends have unhealthy body images, they may spend a lot of time saying negative things about themselves. It can be hard to know what to do or say when a friend insults his own appearance. Saying nothing doesn't feel right. Arguing can feel pointless, and feeling like a friend needs constant reassurance can be exhausting. Self-esteem experts recommend calling out negative comments with loving firmness. If a friend calls himself or herself ugly or fat, Sarah Yankowski, someone in recovery for an eating disorder, says to try comments such as, "Hey, don't talk to my friend that way," or "That's a mean thing to say to my friend."[10] If people become aware that they are being mean or cruel to themselves, they may start to reexamine their own behavior.

its own kind of pain. It can be tempting to give pep talks to people with unhealthy body image, trying to reason them out of their obsessive, negative thoughts. But it's important to recognize that treating mental disorders is a job for mental health professionals. If you suspect that someone in your life is suffering from disordered thinking, eating, or exercise patterns, you can reach out to let them know that they're not alone. Encourage them to talk to someone, such as a parent, guardian, or trusted counselor. Let them know that there is help available and that there is hope that they can get better.

Friends can support others with poor body image by checking in with them to see what they need and by letting them know that they are not alone.

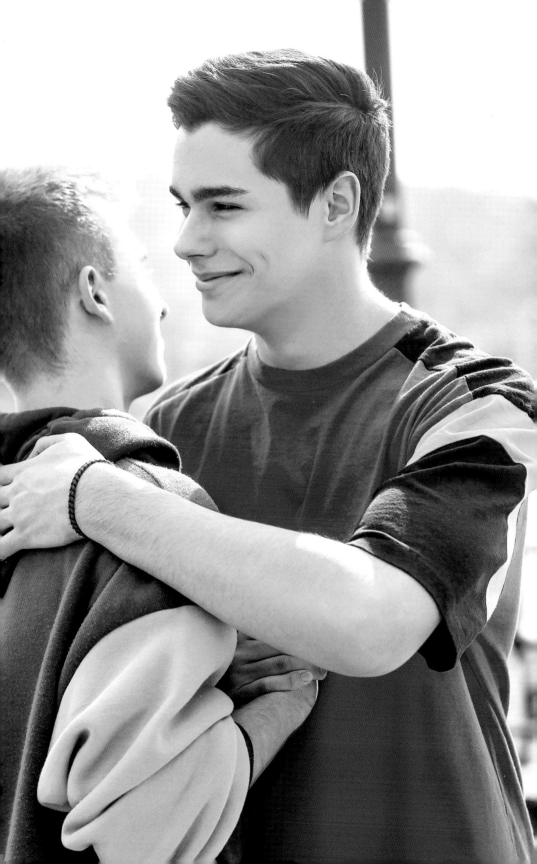

Teens can work on their body images by participating in moderate exercise and activities, such as yoga.

CHAPTER EIGHT

BUILDING A HEALTHY BODY IMAGE

There are resources and strategies available for teens who want to help themselves and others with body acceptance. Becoming more critical of beauty standards and better able to dissect harmful messages in advertising and culture can help teens gain confidence in their own perceptions. For other teens and adults, having a healthy body image can mean rethinking the concept of beauty or rejecting it altogether.

MODELING HEALTHY BODY IMAGE

Parents and educators play a huge role in helping kids begin life with a healthy body image. One of the most important things they can do is set an example for their kids. Karen Diaz is a dietitian and eating coach. She works with eating disorder patients at a treatment center and is the author of a book about how to improve body image within families. Diaz has a key piece of advice for parents who want to help their children with body image. "You have to focus on yourself," Diaz says.[1] Diaz believes that by working through their own issues around body image, parents are better able to be positive role models and caring helpers to their children.

BODY NEUTRALITY

Sometimes, the language of body positivity can feel overpowering. There are plenty of physical and mental health benefits to having a positive, accepting relationship with your own body. But, some critics of positivity point out, it is also normal to not love everything about how your body looks and feels. Occasional negative thoughts aren't necessarily unhealthy. The term *body neutrality* emerged in the 2010s to embrace a new idea of body acceptance without constant positive feelings. Anne Poirier began running workshops on the idea in 2016. Body neutrality's goal is for people to spend less time thinking about their bodies and more time doing other things. It offers a path toward healthy body image by allowing the body to fade into the mental background.

Other experts emphasize the importance of raising children who don't feel defined by their looks. Instead of praising kids' looks, body image expert Renee Engeln recommends spending less time talking about bodies. "A way to help [girls] feel better about their bodies is to talk less about how their bodies look and instead think more about what your body can do, how it feels and where it can take you," Engeln explained in an interview.[2] Pediatric psychologist Jaclyn Shepard also recommends that parents watch the way they talk about other people's bodies. "There's an increase in younger children engaging in dieting behaviors or feeling dissatisfied with their own bodies because they see their parents

"LOVING YOURSELF IS NOT ANTITHETICAL TO HEALTH, IT IS INTRINSIC TO HEALTH. YOU CAN'T TAKE GOOD CARE OF A THING YOU HATE."[4]
—LINDY WEST, AUTHOR AND FAT ACCEPTANCE ACTIVIST

dieting," Shepard says.[3] She recommends that families avoid words like *ugly* and *fat* when used as negative descriptions of other people or of themselves. Refusing to use that language at home helps kids not use that same negative language about their own bodies.

Teachers and role models like coaches can also help kids build healthy senses of body and self. Teachers can play a very important role in stopping appearance-based bullying. According to a 2019 article in *Frontiers in Psychology*, when teachers are open about addressing bullying among kids, they can make a difference in the way kids perceive their behavior. Teachers who win the respect of their students can help reduce in-school bullying. They can become more effective educators and antibullying advocates by learning about body image issues. There are resources available for teachers who want to give lessons on body image. For example, the organization Teaching Tolerance offers body image activities and lessons for students in elementary school through high school. One lesson for elementary schoolers shows teachers how to guide a class discussion about what it means to be healthy and have a healthy body. Children can reflect on the differences between their ideas of a healthy body and the messages they're getting about which bodies are valuable.

CHANGING PERCEPTIONS

Not everyone has healthy body image role models early in life. All people, regardless of upbringing, absorb some of society's toxic images about beauty and body ideals. Learning to understand and challenge beauty standards can soften the myths' power.

Some teens become their own body image educators. Marissa Parks spent her childhood and early teen years with an unhealthy body image. Eventually, she learned about body positivity and started breaking down some of the harmful messages she'd internalized. Parks decided to take the lessons she had learned and share them through a program called the Body Project. The Body Project was developed and tested by researchers Eric Stice, Carolyn Becker Black, and colleagues. Its goal is to give young people a space to talk about and challenge appearance-based messages and beauty standards.

Teachers can model healthy eating and positive body image in their classrooms.

The project includes workshops, guided conversations, and activities to raise awareness of body issues. "Students who went through the program led workshops, put Post-It notes with body-positive phrases on bathroom mirrors and exercise machines, and encouraged informed conversations about body image," Parks wrote.[5] The original version of the Body Project is aimed at girls and women, but researchers have also developed and tested similar programs for boys and men, and specifically for gay and bisexual boys and men. They have called for a more inclusive Body Project that includes those of marginalized gender, racial, and sexual identities.[6]

BODY IMAGE AND PHYSICAL DISABILITY

Having a physical disability can deeply affect the way people relate to their own bodies and to social beauty standards. Raya Al-Jadir has muscular dystrophy, which prevents her from walking, and scoliosis, which curves her spine. She describes loving herself at an early age while also being aware that others saw her as different. Al-Jadir has had to deal with hostile or condescending comments from others throughout her life. Her journey to body acceptance involved being grateful to her body for the personal strength and insight it helped give her.

Other teens and young adults take their criticism of unrealistic beauty standards straight to the source. In 2012, a feminist, anti-racist organization called SPARK Movement protested *Teen Vogue*'s use of digitally altered photos. The process of digitally altering photos is also commonly called retouching or airbrushing. Advertisements and fashion spreads almost always use digitally altered images to change the appearances of models and celebrities. These altered images typically make models represent an unrealistic beauty standard by smoothing their skin, erasing wrinkles from their clothes, removing stray hairs that fall across their faces, increasing breast sizes, increasing muscle definition, and decreasing the sizes of their waists, thighs, and other body parts.

Some digital alterations to photos are large and noticeable, while others, such as removing wrinkles or making someone's fingers longer and thinner, may not be as obvious.

Many body image activists object to airbrushing, arguing that the popularity of these digitally altered photos has a negative effect on our minds. Airbrushing, these activists believe, promotes a standard of beauty that is literally impossible to achieve in real life. In 2012, SPARK Movement activist Julia Bluhm started a petition asking *Seventeen* magazine to use one unairbrushed photo a month in its pages. In response, *Seventeen* published its Body Peace Treaty and swore not to airbrush its models.

BEYOND BEAUTIFUL

For some people, the journey to healthy body image is about learning to feel beautiful. Healthy body image can include embracing traditional ideas about beauty. It can also mean finding a definition of beautiful that is personal and unique. When Harnaam Kaur hit puberty, she began to grow more body hair. Kaur has a condition called polycystic ovary syndrome (PCOS), which can cause additional hair growth. Kaur started growing hair on her face in the pattern of a mustache and beard. At first, she was ashamed of her facial hair and did all she could to shave or hide it. In time, she came to accept that her beard was part of who she was and a unique facet of her body image. Today, Kaur proudly wears her beard, and she works as a model and body acceptance advocate. She even has a tattoo of her own face on her leg—a reminder that she sets her own beauty standard.

Some people find body acceptance in rejecting beauty altogether. Robert Hoge calls himself ugly. But that doesn't mean he doesn't accept his body. Hoge was born with a tumor on his face and leg deformities. After the tumor was removed, he went through several surgeries that left him with a wide, unusually shaped nose and eyes that are very far apart. Hoge's legs were amputated in his childhood too. When Hoge calls himself ugly, sometimes people

"PEOPLE WHO APPRECIATE AND FEEL GRATITUDE TOWARD THEIR BODY ARE *MORE* LIKELY TO TAKE GOOD CARE OF IT."[7]

—*RENEE ENGELN, PSYCHOLOGIST AND BODY IMAGE EXPERT*

interrupt him to say that everyone is beautiful in their own way. That doesn't feel true to him. *Ugly* feels like it describes him, and he finds pride and comfort in his identity. "Ugliness is its own, wonderful thing," Hoge writes.[8]

Hoge has looked different his whole life, and his experiences have helped make him the person he is. He is someone who understands that appearance affects how we live and are treated. But he has also learned not to make assumptions about people based on the way they look. Hoge sees ugliness as part of the diversity of human life, something to accept and be proud of.

"FAT TALK"

Sometimes, girls and women especially put down their own bodies in public or when talking to family and friends. Many people call this "fat talk." Researcher Renee Engeln found that about 90 percent of women engaged in fat talk.[9] Engeln's research shows that girls and women may feel pressured to participate in fat talk even when they don't feel dissatisfaction with their own bodies. Instead, they use fat talk as an attempt to relate to other women. Engeln encourages girls and women to examine the idea that women should act as if they hate their bodies in order to feel comfortable around other people. Fat talk is harmful. For the individual doing the fat talk, it is associated with increased body dissatisfaction, body shame, and disordered eating. Fat talk is also contagious, so when someone does it, others who are around are more likely to participate as well. This potentially increases their body dissatisfaction and body shame as a result.

In 2019, activists at London Fashion Week protested in an effort to see greater representation on the catwalk.

CHAPTER NINE

THE FUTURE OF BODY IMAGE

Teens today are pushing the body image conversation forward. Their roles as consumers, online content creators, entertainers, and activists help evolve society's understanding of what it means to have a healthy or unhealthy body image. In the future, the teens of today will become the businesspeople selling skin-care lines, the teachers preventing body shaming and bullying, the parents teaching their kids about healthy bodies, and the therapists guiding patients toward improved mental health. Some of the body image challenges that teens face are generations old, and others are more specific to the age of social media.

There are two particular areas where teens can play a big role in national conversations about body image. The first is in the area of beauty standards. Thanks in part to the work of teen activists, many companies have embraced wider beauty standards in their advertising and marketing. Representation of people of different

"GETTING A MAN 101"

Jahkara Smith started posting YouTube videos at age 21. Her videos were funny, ironic takes on YouTube makeup tutorials, where she mocked gender- and race-based beauty standards while putting on a full face of makeup. In a video called "GETTING A MAN 101," her advice starts, "The first thing you want to do is hide the fact that you have human flesh." Smith, who is Black, mocks white beauty standards by sarcastically saying, "If you don't look like a white beauty blogger, it's over for you." Smith gained a following of over 500,000 subscribers by showcasing her approach to makeup while still being critical of beauty myths.[1]

body types, skin colors, backgrounds, and identities on TV and in magazines can send an empowering message to teens. But it can also encourage a narrow focus on appearance. Today's teens can work on both sides of the beauty standards conversation, expanding standards and finding ways to live outside them.

In addition, teen creators are making names for themselves on platforms such as YouTube and TikTok, alongside older media like music and TV. With public attention often comes objectification, sometimes on a large and disturbing scale. Teen creators and public figures are fighting for the right to display and embrace their bodies without being objectified. And they're using innovative tactics to stand up for their right to define their own body images.

BODY-INCLUSIVE MEDIA AND ADVERTISING

In the 1990s and 2000s, long before SPARK Movement sent its petition to *Seventeen* magazine, Victoria's Secret was the biggest name in women's underwear. The brand was famous for its annual Angels show, where the biggest names in modeling walked the runway in the company's latest styles. Models spoke of having to starve themselves ahead of the show. One repeat model said that she didn't eat solid food for nine days before walking. Until 2019, Victoria's Secret had never used a plus-size model.

By that time, however, Victoria's Secret was losing market share to a new generation of companies. Its rival, Aerie, makes underwear and clothing for teens and women. It stopped using Photoshop in its ads in 2014. The company listened to activists calling for models of a variety of shapes, sizes, looks, and abilities in its ads. In 2014, it launched a successful multiyear campaign called #AerieREAL,

"AS FAR AS THE INDUSTRY GOES, I THINK IF WE CONTINUE TO . . . MAKE IT VERY INCLUSIVE BEHIND THE SCENES AND IN FRONT OF THE SCENES, IT'S GOING TO DEFINITELY HELP THE INDUSTRY MOVE VERY, VERY FORWARD."[2]

—*JILLIAN MERCADO, MODEL WITH MUSCULAR DYSTROPHY AND WHEELCHAIR USER*

In January 2020, #AerieREAL models including Ali Stroker, *center*, attended Aerie's An Evening of Change event in New York City.

featuring models from all walks of life. Ali Stroker is a Tony Award-winning actress and wheelchair user who modeled in an Aerie campaign. She talked about what seeing someone like her model might have meant to her younger self. "When I was growing up," Stroker recalls, "I didn't see anyone like me modeling the clothes that I loved to wear." During the campaign, Stroker said she believes in "turning limitations into opportunities."[3]

However, there are limits to the horizons that companies such as Aerie have expanded. Centering discussions of body positivity around women's underwear can help send the message that buying lingerie is still an important step to having the correct appearance. And companies such as Aerie and Dove still focus their body image conversations around people who buy women's products rather than considering people of all genders.

BEYOND OBJECTIFICATION

Billie Eilish had a huge year in 2019. She was 17 years old when her debut album, *When We All Fall Asleep, Where Do We Go?*, became a runaway hit. At the 2020 Grammys, Eilish took home five awards and became the youngest person ever to win a Grammy for Best New Album.[4]

Eilish has opened up about her struggle with body image issues while being a young female celebrity. At a 2020 concert, Eilish played a video clip that expressed her frustration with the pressures she was under. In the voice-over for the video, Eilish said:

> "I'VE NEVER FELT COMFORTABLE IN REALLY TINY CLOTHES. I WAS ALWAYS WORRIED ABOUT MY APPEARANCE."[5]
> —*BILLIE EILISH, SINGER, ON HER BODY IMAGE*

> *Some people hate what I wear, some people praise it. Some people use it to shame others, some people use it to shame me. . . . Would you like me to be smaller? Weaker? Softer? Taller? . . . Though you've never seen my body, you . . . judge me for it. Why?*[6]

BODY IMAGE AND VIRTUAL REALITY

The world of virtual reality allows people to explore digital worlds in a body that may look very different from their own. More research is needed on the effect of digital alter egos on a person's real-life body image. For instance, people who use the virtual reality (VR) program VRChat interact with other real people using digital avatars, or substitute bodies. These bodies can look like people, animals, or cartoon characters. Users have the chance to design their avatars inside the program. These avatars can reflect a user's self-image, their fantasies, or a mix of both. Virtual reality may have therapeutic uses as well. Some evidence shows that virtual reality can help eating disorder patients with perceptual body image. A 2016 study showed that showing anorexia patients virtual models of their own bodies helped them have a more accurate perception of their body size.

Sometimes, the road to body acceptance can start with the realization that you don't need to look a certain way to have fun and connect with others. Annie Pham is a high school student who likes making TikTok videos in her spare time. In August 2019, she uploaded a video making fun of the trend of "glow-up" TikToks, where users show themselves before and after applying makeup and dressing themselves perfectly. In the video, Pham, barefaced and in a gray shirt, pretends not to understand why she hasn't magically transformed into her hottest, most perfect self. "Why isn't it working?" she cries at the end of the video. Pham's video got over 800,000 likes

Billie Eilish is known for her eclectic style and body positivity.

from other users who connected to her sense of humor, not the idealized self missing from the end of the video. And Pham, who continues to share her work on social media, felt a sense of connection as well. "I was reading the comments," Pham told Vox. "And it was really cool to see how much people relate to it."[7]

While negative body image is a problem for many teens, positive role models such as Stroker, Eilish, and Pham show others how to appreciate their bodies and live healthful, happy lives. Teens can encourage each other to speak out against negativity and connect with like-minded people to build support networks. Societal standards for what bodies "should" look like will continue to change, but teens can help each other stay positive and accept their bodies for what they are.

FACTS ABOUT BODY IMAGE AND DYSMORPHIA

- Body image refers to the way we perceive our bodies, the thoughts and feelings we have about our bodies, and the way we treat our bodies.

- Body image is shaped by early experiences as well as cultural messages called beauty standards.

- Body image can be healthy or unhealthy. People with healthy body image accept their appearance the way it is.

- Body dysmorphic disorder (BDD) is an illness defined by obsessive, negative thoughts and feelings about appearance. It is a life-threatening illness that can have a severe impact on a person's ability to live a healthy, fulfilling life.

IMPACT ON DAILY LIFE

- Approximately 25 percent of US teen boys and 50 to 80 percent of teen girls feel negatively about their bodies.

- Approximately 2 to 3 percent of people in the United States develop BDD. The symptoms of the disorder usually start in the teen years.

- Teens with negative body image may experience poorer physical and mental health. They may also miss out on important life events and opportunities to connect with others.

DEALING WITH BODY IMAGE AND DYSMORPHIA

- Effective treatments for BDD include talk therapy, such as cognitive behavioral therapy, and medication.

- A healthy diet, moderate exercise, and a positive, self-accepting attitude help maintain good body image.

- Today's teens are innovating new ways to deal with the pressures of objectification and shifting beauty standards.

QUOTE

"One of my most significant realizations is that changing my body does not mean I will automatically love myself. I have learned that self-love and body image have far more to do with my mental state than my physical appearance."

—*Emily Locke, blogger*

GLOSSARY

bodybuilder
Someone who builds muscle for competitions based on muscle size and appearance.

cognitive
Related to the act or process of thinking, reasoning, remembering, imagining, or learning.

comorbid
Describing two or more illnesses or disorders occurring in the same person at the same time.

detoxify
To remove harmful substances.

laxative
A type of medication that causes someone to have bowel movements.

market share
The percentage of the overall market that one company has.

mental disorder
An illness that mainly affects thoughts, feelings, and mental processes.

nonbinary

Having a gender identity that is neither male nor female.

relapse

A return to prior, unhealthy behaviors after a period of recovery.

status symbol

An object or trait that demonstrates wealth and power to others.

stigmatize

To create an unfair, negative belief about someone or something.

talk therapy

A treatment for psychological disorders involving regular sessions talking with a psychiatrist or therapist.

ADDITIONAL RESOURCES

SELECTED BIBLIOGRAPHY

American Psychiatric Association. *Diagnostic and Statistical Manual of Mental Disorders*. American Psychiatric Pub, 2013.

Engeln, Renee. *Beauty Sick: How the Cultural Obsession with Appearance Hurts Girls and Women*. HarperCollins, 2017.

Neziroglu, F., et al. *Overcoming Body Dysmorphic Disorder: A Cognitive Behavioral Approach to Reclaiming Your Life*. New Harbinger Publications, 2012.

FURTHER READINGS

Huddleston, Emma. *Nutrition and Exercise*. Abdo, 2021.

Lusted, Marcia Amidon. *Puberty*. Abdo, 2022.

Morgan, Nicola. *Body Brilliant: A Teenage Guide to a Positive Body Image*. Hachette UK, 2019.

ONLINE RESOURCES

To learn more about body image and dysmorphia, please visit **abdobooklinks.com** or scan this QR code. These links are routinely monitored and updated to provide the most current information available.

MORE INFORMATION

For more information on this subject, contact or visit the following organizations:

Body Dysmorphic Disorder Foundation

bddfoundation.org

The Body Dysmorphic Disorder (BDD) Foundation is a UK-based organization that offers resources and information for BDD sufferers. It also advocates for BDD education and treatment.

National Alliance on Mental Illness

4301 Wilson Blvd., Ste. 300
Arlington, VA 22203
nami.org

The National Alliance on Mental Illness (NAMI) is a mental health advocacy organization. NAMI offers education on mental disorders and advocates for laws and regulations to advance the cause of mental health.

National Eating Disorders Association

1500 Broadway, Ste. 1101
New York, NY 10036
nationaleatingdisorders.org

The National Eating Disorders Association (NEDA) offers support, education, and resources to eating disorder sufferers. It also offers a great deal of information about body image and educational tools about building healthy body image.

SOURCE NOTES

CHAPTER 1. THE PERSON IN THE MIRROR

1. Faith Brar and Kelly Mickle. "Demi Lovato's Health and Fitness Journey Will Seriously Inspire You." *Shape*, 24 July 2019, shape.com. Accessed 6 Aug. 2020.
2. Julia Carrie Wong. "How Flat Tummy Co Gamed Instagram to Sell Women the Unattainable Ideal." *Guardian*, 29 Aug. 2018, theguardian.com. Accessed 6 Aug. 2020.
3. Rachel Mosely. "Amandla Stenberg on Being Proud of Her Sexuality." *Seventeen*, 19 Sept. 2018, seventeen.com. Accessed 6 Aug. 2020.
4. Jake Linardon. "The Ultimate List of Body Image Statistics." *Break Binge Eating*, 7 Jan. 2020, breakbingeeating.com. Accessed 6 Aug. 2020.
5. Linardon, "The Ultimate List of Body Image Statistics."
6. "Body Dysmorphic Disorder." *Anxiety and Depression Association of America*, n.d., adaa.org. Accessed 6 Aug. 2020.

CHAPTER 2. HOW BODY IMAGE FORMS

1. Philippe Rochat. "Five Levels of Self-Awareness as They Unfold Early in Life." *Consciousness and Cognition*, 12, 2003. 717–731.
2. Sharita L. Forrest. "Preschoolers Form Body Images—but Parents Are Unaware, Study Says." *Illinois News Bureau*, 5 Oct. 2016, news.illinois.edu. Accessed 6 Aug. 2020.
3. Forrest, "Preschoolers Form Body Images."
4. Clara Mockdece Neves et al. "Body Image in Childhood." *Revista Paulista de Pediatria*, 35, no. 2, 2017. 331–339.
5. "Teeth Whitening Products Market Size Worth USD 7.40 Billion by 2024: Hexa Research." *PR Newswire*, 20 Sept. 2017, prnewswire.com. Accessed 6 Aug. 2020.
6. Jerica M. Berge et al. "Do Parents or Siblings Engage in More Negative Weight-Based Talk with Children and What Does It Sound Like?" *Body Image*, 18, September 2016. 27–33.
7. "Crest 3D White Whitestrips TV Commercial, 'Tissue Test.'" *iSpot.tv*, 2018, ispot.tv. Accessed 6 Aug. 2020.
8. Amanda Mull. "Why Does Everyone Suddenly Have Fancy Fake Teeth?" *Atlantic*, 4 Feb. 2019, theatlantic.com. Accessed 6 Aug. 2020.
9. Robin Givhan. "The Idea of Beauty Is Always Shifting. Today, It's More Inclusive than Ever." *National Geographic*, 7 Jan. 2020, nationalgeographic.com. Accessed 6 Aug. 2020.

CHAPTER 3. BODY IMAGE AND TEENS

1. Jake Linardon. "The Ultimate List of Body Image Statistics." *Break Binge Eating*, 7 Jan. 2020, breakbingeeating.com. Accessed 6 Aug. 2020.
2. "Eating Disorder Facts and Statistics." *The Body Image Therapy Center*, n.d., thebodyimagecenter.com. Accessed 7 Aug. 2020.

3. Naomi Wolf. *The Beauty Myth*. HarperCollins, 2002. 230.

4. Emily Wilson. "A Quick Reminder . . . The Beauty Myth." *Guardian*, 18 Oct. 2005, theguardian.com. Accessed 7 Aug. 2020.

5. Beth Dreher. "What Is the Pink Tax?" *Good Housekeeping*, 23 May 2019, goodhousekeeping.com. Accessed 7 Aug. 2020.

6. Renee Engeln. "Dove's Latest Body Positivity Failure." *Psychology Today*, 15 June 2017, psychologytoday.com. Accessed 7 Aug. 2020.

7. Jamie Santa Cruz. "Body-Image Pressure Increasingly Affects Boys." *Atlantic*, 10 Mar. 2014, theatlantic.com. Accessed 7 Aug. 2020.

8. Jason M. Nagata et al. "Predictors of Muscularity-Oriented Disordered Eating Behaviors." *International Journal of Eating Disorders*, 52, no. 12, Dec. 2019. 1380–1388.

9. "QuickFacts." *United States Census Bureau*, n.d., census.gov. Accessed 7 Aug. 2020.

10. Darnell Hunt et al. "Hollywood Diversity Report 2019." *UCLA College of Social Sciences*, 2019, socialsciences.ucla.edu. Accessed 7 Aug. 2020.

11. Lanetra Bennett. "Local Teen Told Afro Is 'Extreme' and Can't Be Worn at School." *WCTV*, 19 May 2017, wctv.tv. Accessed 7 Aug. 2020.

12. Nicquel Terry Ellis and Charisse Jones. "Banning Ethnic Hairstyles 'Upholds this Notion of White Supremacy.' States Pass Laws to Stop Natural Hair Discrimination." *USA Today*, 14 Oct. 2019, usatoday.com. Accessed 7 Aug. 2020.

13. Christina Newberry. "37 Instagram Stats that Matter to Marketers in 2020." *Hootsuite*, 22 Oct. 2019, blog.hootsuite.com. Accessed 7 Aug. 2020.

14. Leah Donnella. "Is Beauty in the Eyes of the Colonizer?" *Code Switch*, 6 Feb. 2019, npr.org. Accessed 7 Aug. 2020.

15. Monica Anderson. "A Majority of Teens Have Experienced Some Form of Cyberbullying." *Pew Research Center*, 27 Sept. 2018, pewresearch.org. Accessed 7 Aug. 2020.

16. Allure. "Girls Age 6–18 Talk about Body Image." *YouTube*, 31 May 2018, youtube.com. Accessed 7 Aug. 2020.

CHAPTER 4. BODY DYSMORPHIC DISORDER

1. American Psychiatric Association. *Diagnostic and Statistical Manual of Mental Disorders*. American Psychiatric Pub, 2013. 244.

2. "Personal Stories." *Body Dysmorphic Disorder Foundation*, n.d., bddfoundation.org. Accessed 7 Aug. 2020.

3. American Psychiatric Association, *Diagnostic and Statistical Manual of Mental Disorders*, 242.

4. Jennifer L. Greenberg et al. "The Phenomenology of Self-Reported Body Dysmorphic Disorder by Proxy." *Body Image*, 10, no. 2, Mar. 2013. 243–246.

5. "Personal Stories."

6. "Paul's Story." *BDD—Seeing It through Our Eyes*, 9 Jan. 2013, bddseeingitthroughoureyes.com.au. Accessed 7 Aug. 2020.

CHAPTER 5. BDD AND OTHER CONDITIONS

1. "Personal Stories." *Body Dysmorphic Disorder Foundation*, n.d., bddfoundation.org. Accessed 7 Aug. 2020.
2. Jake Gammon. "Multi-Country Study Finds Body Image Improves with Age." *YouGov*, 21 July 2015, today.yougov.com. Accessed 7 Aug. 2020.

CHAPTER 6. THE EFFECTS OF UNHEALTHY BODY IMAGE

1. New York Times. "I Was the Fastest Girl in America, Until I Joined Nike | NYT Opinion." *YouTube*, 7 Nov. 2019, youtube.com. Accessed 7 Aug. 2020.
2. Allure. "Girls Age 6–18 Talk about Body Image." *YouTube*, 31 May 2018, youtube.com. Accessed 7 Aug. 2020.
3. "Girls on Beauty: New Dove Research Finds Low Beauty Confidence Driving 8 in 10 Girls to Opt Out of Future Opportunities." *PR Newswire*, 5 Oct. 2017, prnewswire.org. Accessed 7 Aug. 2020.
4. "Girls on Beauty."
5. Patrick Ferris. "Body Love." *Rookie*, 22 Jan. 2018, rookiemag.com. Accessed 7 Aug. 2020.
6. Kristina Rodulfo. "Talking Body: Miss Universe Canada Siera Bearchell Is Done with Trying to Be Pageant Skinny." *Elle*, 23 Feb. 2017, elle.com. Accessed 7 Aug. 2020.

CHAPTER 7. TREATMENT OPTIONS

1. S. Higgins and A. Wysong. "Cosmetic Surgery and Body Dysmorphic Disorder." *International Journal of Women's Dermatology*, 4, no. 1, Mar. 2018. 43–48.
2. "How Is BDD Treated?" *International OCD Foundation*, n.d., bdd.iocdf.org. Accessed 7 Aug. 2020.
3. Johanna Linde et al. "Acceptance-Based Exposure Therapy for Body Dysmorphic Disorder: A Pilot Study." *Behavioral Therapy*, 46, no. 4, July 2015. 423–431.
4. "Medication Treatment for BDD: FAQ." *International OCD Foundation*, n.d., bdd. iocdf.org. Accessed 7 Aug. 2020.
5. Ana Sandoiu. "How Can Exercise Improve Body Image?" *Medical News Today*, 18 June 2017, medicalnewstoday.com. Accessed 7 Aug. 2020.
6. "Health at Every Size Approach." *Association for Size Diversity and Health*, n.d., sizediversityandhealth.org. Accessed 7 Aug. 2020.
7. Emily Locke. "Summer of Self-Love." *National Eating Disorders Association*, 2018, nationaleatingdisorders.org. Accessed 7 Aug. 2020.
8. Louise Green. "Here's How the 'Health at Every Size' Movement Made Me a Better Trainer." *Self*, 9 Jan. 2020, self.com. Accessed 7 Aug. 2020.
9. "Why Should I Get Treatment?" *International OCD Foundation*, n.d., bdd.iocdf.org. Accessed 7 Aug. 2020.
10. Sarah Lauren Yankowski. "A Recovering Bulimic's Guide to Self Love." *Odyssey*, 18 Oct. 2016, theodysseyonline.com. Accessed 7 Aug. 2020.

CHAPTER 8. BUILDING A HEALTHY BODY IMAGE

1. "Healing Generational Food & Body Image Issues with Karen Diaz." *Body Image Podcast*, created by Corinne Dobbas, season 2, episode 15, Body Image Podcast, 2019.
2. Maria Volkova. "Through the Looking Glass: Are We Mirroring Our Mother's Body Image?" *Blood & Milk*, 31 May 2018, bloodandmilk.com. Accessed 7 Aug. 2020.
3. Megan Davis. "5 Ways to Help Kids Build a Healthy Body Image." *UVA Health*, 16 June 2016, blog.uvahealth.com. Accessed 7 Aug. 2020.
4. Lindy West. *Shrill*. Hachette Book Group, 2016. 103.
5. Marissa Parks. "How I Became a Body Image Activist through 'The Body Project.'" *National Eating Disorders Association*, 2018, nationaleatingdisorders.org. Accessed 7 Aug. 2020.
6. Tiffany A. Brown et al. "A Randomized Controlled Trial of the Body Project: More than Muscles for Men with Body Dissatisfaction." *International Journal of Eating Disorders*, 50, no. 8, Aug. 2017. 873–883.
7. Renee Engeln. "What We're Getting Wrong about 'Positive Body Image.'" *Psychology Today*, 23 Mar. 2019, psychologytoday.com. Accessed 7 Aug. 2020.
8. Robert Hoge. "5 Things I've Learned from Being 'Ugly.'" *Time*, 6 Sept. 2016, time.com. Accessed 7 Aug. 2020.
9. Renee Engeln. "The Problem with 'Fat Talk.'" *New York Times*, 13 Mar. 2015, nytimes.com. Accessed 7 Aug. 2020.

CHAPTER 9. THE FUTURE OF BODY IMAGE

1. Valeriya Safronova. "Air Force by Day, YouTube by Night." *New York Times*, 14 May 2018, nytimes.com. Accessed 7 Aug. 2020.
2. NowThis Entertainment. "How Beyoncé & Target Model Jillian Mercado Is Normalizing Disabilities in Fashion | NowThis." *YouTube*, 9 July 2019, youtube.com. Accessed 7 Aug. 2020.
3. Sarah Kim. "Aerie Continues to Include Authentic Disability Representation— Ali Stroker Joins #AerieREAL Role Model Family." *Forbes*, 31 Jan. 2020, forbes.com. Accessed 7 Aug. 2020.
4. "Billie Eilish at the Grammys: A Timeline of Her Life and Career." *BBC*, 27 Jan. 2020, bbc.co.uk. Accessed 7 Aug. 2020.
5. Josh Eells. "She's a 17-Year-Old Superstar Who Did It Her Way and Doesn't Care What You Think—Even If She Still Calls Out for Mom after a Bad Dream." *Rolling Stone*, 31 July 2019, rollingstone.com. Accessed 7 Aug. 2020.
6. Laura Snapes. "'If I Shed the Layers, I Am a Slut': Billie Eilish Addresses Body Image Criticism." *Irish Times*, 11 Mar. 2020, irishtimes.com. Accessed 7 Aug. 2020.
7. Rebecca Jennings. "Teens are Calling Themselves 'Ugly' on TikTok. It's Not as Depressing as You Think." *Vox*, 14 Nov. 2019, vox.com. Accessed 7 Aug. 2020.

INDEX

ABOUT THE AUTHOR

A. W. BUCKEY

A. W. Buckey is a writer and petsitter living in Brooklyn, New York.

ABOUT THE CONSULTANT

D. C. WALKER

D. C. Walker is an assistant professor of psychology at Union College, a liberal arts college in Schenectady, New York. Dr. Walker is also a licensed clinical psychologist and conducts individual and group therapy in Albany, New York. Dr. Walker's research and clinical practice focus on body image as well as eating disorder prevention and treatment.